# Cesar Chavez
## Latino American Civil Rights Activist

**by Grace Hansen**

Abdo
**HISTORY MAKER BIOGRAPHIES**
Kids

**abdopublishing.com**

Published by Abdo Kids, a division of ABDO, PO Box 398166, Minneapolis, Minnesota 55439.

Copyright © 2016 by Abdo Consulting Group, Inc. International copyrights reserved in all countries. No part of this book may be reproduced in any form without written permission from the publisher.

Printed in the United States of America, North Mankato, Minnesota.

102015

012016

THIS BOOK CONTAINS
RECYCLED MATERIALS

Photo Credits: AP Images, Cesar Chavez Foundation, Corbis, Getty Images, iStock, Shutterstock

Production Contributors: Teddy Borth, Jennie Forsberg, Grace Hansen

Design Contributors: Laura Mitchell, Dorothy Toth

Library of Congress Control Number: 2015941765

Cataloging-in-Publication Data

Hansen, Grace.

 Cesar Chavez: Latino American civil rights activist / Grace Hansen.

  p. cm. -- (History maker biographies)

Includes index.

ISBN 978-1-68080-122-4

1. Chavez, Cesar, 1927-1993--Juvenile literature.  2. Labor leaders--United States--Biography--Juvenile literature.  3. United Farm Workers--Juvenile literature.  4. Mexican American migrant agricultural laborers--Biography--Juvenile literature.  1. Title.

331.88/13/092--dc23

[B]

2015941765

# Table of Contents

## Early Life

Cesar Chavez was born on March 31, 1927. He grew up near Yuma, Arizona. His family had a farm.

Arizona

5

Cesar's parents were from Mexico. They came to the United States before he was born. They taught him to help the less **fortunate**.

Cesar's family lost their farm when he was 11. They moved to California for work. They became **migrant** farmworkers.

## Taking a Stand

Farmwork was very hard.
Workers had long hours. They
were paid very little. They did
not get breaks or clean water.

11

Farmworkers needed rights. Cesar's dream was to set up a **union**. This union would protect farmworkers.

13

In 1952, Cesar got a great job. This job let him help **immigrants**. He was happy with his work. But he still wanted to help farmworkers.

15

In 1962, Cesar started the National Farm Workers Association (NFWA). It asked farm owners to make better working conditions. Many refused. Cesar used **boycotts** and protests to make change happen.

Years later, Cesar was seeing progress. Farmworkers were getting fairer treatment. They got breaks and clean water. They had better pay and much more.

18

19

## Death & Legacy

Cesar spent his life helping the poorest people. He taught farmworkers about their rights. And he worked hard to get them those rights. He died on April 23, 1993.

# Timeline

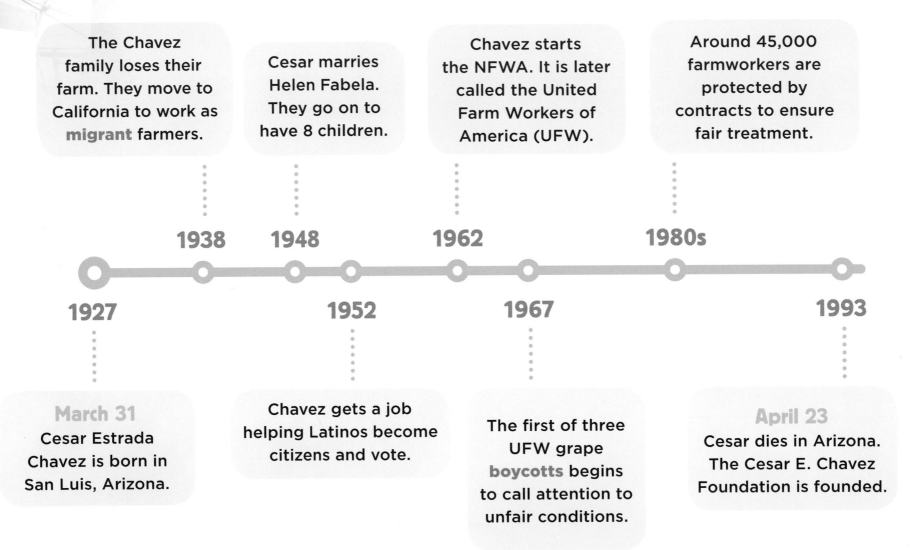

The Chavez family loses their farm. They move to California to work as **migrant** farmers.

Cesar marries Helen Fabela. They go on to have 8 children.

Chavez starts the NFWA. It is later called the United Farm Workers of America (UFW).

Around 45,000 farmworkers are protected by contracts to ensure fair treatment.

**1938** **1948** **1962** **1980s**

**1927** **1952** **1967** **1993**

**March 31**
Cesar Estrada Chavez is born in San Luis, Arizona.

Chavez gets a job helping Latinos become citizens and vote.

The first of three UFW grape **boycotts** begins to call attention to unfair conditions.

**April 23**
Cesar dies in Arizona. The Cesar E. Chavez Foundation is founded.

# Glossary

**boycott** – an act of joining with others to ban a certain person, product, place, or organization.

**fortunate** – lucky.

**immigrant** – a person who moves to a new country to live.

**migrant** – a person who moves from place to place to find work.

**union** – an organized group of workers who come together to impact their wages, hours, health, safety, and other work-related issues.

# Index

## abdokids.com

Use this code to log on to abdokids.com and access crafts, games, videos, and more!

Abdo Kids Code:
HCK1224

24

05/2016